PUTTING THE VISIBLE
IN SO CALLED
INVISIBLE ILLNESSES
THROUGH POETRY

Table of Contents

Stinks (Like Manure)

In my teens I was athletic
Now I feel pathetic
Always seeming to be apologetic
And hardly ever energetic
But trying to make my thoughts poetic.

My appetite can be described as choosy
My drink is never boozy
Ensuring that my head is never fuzzy
Although at times it can be muzzy
As my thoughts turn bluesy.

I try to stay demure
Instead I come over obscure.
My heart and my intentions are pure
I know this, even if others are unsure.
For my condition there is no cure
The fact no painkiller works makes me dour
Now the friends I have are even fewer
Life stinks (like manure)

A tight chest makes me wheeze
Anxiety makes it harder to breathe

My joints often lock and seize
With pain that never seems to ease.
Tasks that were easy are no longer a breeze.

There is no release.
There is no peace.
Although the pain may decrease.
It will never cease.
It will never cease.

I try to stay demure
Instead I come over obscure.
My heart and my intentions are pure
I know this, even if others are unsure.

For my condition there is no cure
The fact no painkiller works makes me dour
Now the friends I have are even fewer
Life stinks (like manure)

I hate people who schmooze
Fake sincerity they do ooze
This life I did not choose!
My patience I tend to lose
Until I completely blow a fuse.

I don't smoke or booze
I don't rely upon regular brews
Nor do I have an addiction to shoes
Bags, however, my plastic I will abuse.
Afternoons I prefer to snooze.

I try to stay demure
Instead I come over obscure.
My heart and my intentions are pure
I know this, even if others are unsure.

For my condition there is no cure
The fact no painkiller works makes me dour
Now the friends I have are even fewer
Life stinks (like manure)

Mirror

The girl in the mirror isn't you
Bags under her eyes a purple hue
Skin white as morning dew
The girl in the mirror isn't you.

The girl in the mirror isn't you.
The reflection you see lies to you
Imperfections highlighted though they are few
The girl in the mirror isn't you.

The reflection you see lies to you
Your inner strength can't shine through
You can battle this too.
What you see isn't you.

Scrapes and scars that are new
Fade in time - phew
A normal face gives no clue
Of what you are going through.

The colour of your world is blue
Giving up is all you want to do
But don't!; don't believe it to be true
The girl in the mirror isn't you.

Fear

Fear of what we will be
Of what we should flee.
Fear of what bites us next
Fear of what is in the subtext.

Fear of helplessness consuming us.
Fear of helplessness we must suss.
Fear of our hopes being eroded for good
Fear of our hopes not being what they should.

Fear of everlasting darkness
Of everlasting starkness.
Of never ending pain
Fear of never ending rain.

Fear of nobody understanding
Of everyone demanding.
Fear ever consuming
Ever blooming.

Fear dictating where we go and what we see
Dictating who are we.
Fear bellowing, like a fire breathing lizard
Swirling our ears like a blizzard.

Fear that nothing will be the same again
That nothing will ever remain.
Fear that we will never adjust
Fear that we must.

Fear of losing our loved ones
Of losing tonnes.
Fear of causing pain to our family
Fear of causing a tragedy.

Fear of driving away that trusted only friend
Of driving away a hand you'd readily lend.
Of being alone but swept away by the crowd.
Of speaking up because we are proud.

Fear of never recovering.
Fear of it smothering.
Fear of it returning.
Fear of it burning.

Fear of no longer coping
Of no longer hoping.
Fear that minor things are worse
Fear that upon you there is a curse.

Fear that it's life changing
That it's real, not gaming.
Fear that it's life threatening
Fear that is so unsettling.

Fear tells us to stop the battle.
Tells us to stop the prattle.
Fear fills our ears with addle.
Fills our heads with tittle-tattle.

Fear that mocks our efforts and talks
That mocks our shadow and stalks.
Fear that chases away our dreams
That extinguishes grand schemes.

Fear that lingers everywhere
That lingers without a care.
Fear that in the end no justice will be served
Fear that off the right road we will be swerved.

Fear that we are not enough
That we are not as tough.
Fear that life now is too rough.
That our resolve will turn to fluff.

Fear overrules common sense
Overrules intelligence
Fear overrules coping strategies
Overrules dreams and fantasies.

Fear that takes over our thoughts
Fear that hurts us lots.
Fear must be quashed.

Fear must be eradicated.
Fear must never be vindicated.
Fear must be destroyed.

Never again our emotions be toyed.
Never again must be in control
Never again must enter your soul.

Apologies

Apologies stick in your throat like a fish bone.
Apologies go very badly in the wrong tone.
Apologies are harder to crack than granite.
The hardest thing to utter on this planet.

Apologies dismissed with the wave of a hand.
But did you listen; did you even understand?
Apologies are difficult for everyone.
But nobody is perfect, everyone makes some.

Get it over with and move on!

My apologies that you lost the thread
Of what was being said.
My apologies you don't get my dulcet tones
Embarrassed, I'm shuddering to my bones.

My apologies to you, and you, and yours.

Apologies that are demanded
As you are reprimanded
Tend to be quick and insincere
And leave us all feeling queer.

Stuttering, stumbling, whispering or mumbling
Once apology's out, it can't be taken back.
This flies also for an insult or comment,
virtually anything considered a personal attack.

Grudge holding
Looks of scolding
Cold shoulders and ignoring
Can be equally provoking.

Get it over with and move on.

Of All The Things

Of all the things
You've given me
Love and Sweet nothings
And much more, you'll see.

Of all the things
You've given me
A reason to believe
Reassurance it's okay to grieve

Of all the things
you've given me
A reason to thrive
And feel so alive.

Of all the things
You've given me
A reason to breathe
And not to leave

Of all the things
You've given me
A reason to smile
And stay awhile.

Of all the things
You've given me
A reason to try
And not just to cry.

Of all the things
You've given me
A reason to hope
A lifeline rope.

Of all the things
You've given me
Strength and sense
With no pretence

Of all the things
You've given me
I'm so grateful
This I hope you see.

My Interests

Second honeymoon in Venice
Yearly tickets for the tennis
But I make no premise
Sometimes my condition is a menace

It seems I have come to an impasse.
Life is art, expressed on a canvas.
Not bright as gold, but maybe brass.
Until an offensive comment from a smartass
Smashes my inner peace like glass.

Just as it evens out, my life gets rougher
I'm starting to think I'm meant to suffer
A failing memory makes me a good bluffer
I have, before my time, become an old huffer.
Perhaps it's all a lesson to make me tougher.

In town I am a minor celeb.
To others I am just a pleb.
Strength tends to flow and ebb.
Like a spider creating another web.

Normal Life is an enigma
There's always an extra dilemma

Wavering energy affect my stamina
Requiring a flexible agenda.

Just as it evens out, my life gets rougher
I'm starting to think I'm meant to suffer
A failing memory makes me a good bluffer
I have, before my time, become an old huffer.
Perhaps it's all a lesson to make me tougher.

I still love to use my camera
My sugar choice is Demerara
Sometimes I'm hot like in the Sahara
My perfume is lighter than Samsara.

I love hot chocolate from Caffè Nero
I have a Steiff lion called Leo
This summer I've watched Olympics from Rio
When interests in other projects were zero.

Just as it evens out, my life gets rougher
I'm starting to think I'm meant to suffer
A failing memory makes me a good bluffer
I have, before my time, become an old huffer.
Perhaps it's all a lesson to make me tougher.

Rattles the China

Unwell, I shivered
But nobody is mithered.
Downstairs I have slithered.
Waiting for the parcel to be delivered
Finding the note of minutes before - package
undelivered.
On my lips the swear word quivered.

It doesn't take much to get me in a tizzy
I can't stomach liquids that are fizzy
Sitting up too fast turns me dizzy
So much to do, I'm always busy.

Did I mention
I'm full of stress and tension
Anxiety and apprehension
My worries don't recede, they only strengthen.

Joints pulling out of their socket
Pain fires through me like a rocket
Vital medication kept in my pocket
With the updated patient docket
In case, for some reason, I cop it.

My tremor rattles the china
The latest of my issues is angina
Silence in my head screams like a Myna
Oh to escape somewhere like South Carolina.
Where the weather and people are finer.

Did I mention
I'm full of stress and tension
Anxiety and apprehension
My worries don't recede, they only strengthen.

Befuddle Double

I'm not great with numbers, better with words
As a result I got on best with the nerds.
I speak with the animals and the birds
Crowds are driven around in herds
I think pavements should be split into thirds
I have no problem eating curds
As long as they do not look like turds

More than one thing at a time puts me in a muddle
Some people say I'm just trouble
Because I am so easy to befuddle
Behind closed doors I try to keep my struggle
Minimise the pain quickly, on the double.

But life is falling around me like rubble
Tears forming a huge puddle
Problems prickly like stubble
So many things at once to juggle
No wonder I retreat into my bubble.
In bed with my boys I snuggle
Reassurance as warm as an everlasting cuddle.

Sports, Games and Hobbies

My life is a decathlon.
Although I'm a simpleton.
Trying to catch up like in the chasing peleton.
Juggling more balls than Wimbledon.
Things happen in threes like with Triathlon.

A previous national team member for Judo
Staying in with family, playing Cluedo and Ludo
Days out and walks with my beau
Until, uh-oh, I'm laid low
And all activities I have to forgo.

I'll watch sports, except cricket
There my interest is split
As I colour and write with wit
Or chalk up some mileage on a FitBit.
(or too tired to do anything but submit)

My time for thinking used to be while running
Or in the garden, snipping and sunning
Now I'm left in dire straits
Can't move until the pain abates.
No longer can I go out with mates.

I'm in it for the long haul,
Sometimes I can't do bugger all.
Watching the TV's Football or Baseball
Dreaming of days in shopping malls
And nights listening in concert halls.

Colour Relaxation is my new meditation
Rest when I can and take medication
Using the magic trick of my favourite music
Hill walking aided by walking stick
All of this in combination makes up my self
preservation.

Wedding

Wedding Checklist

Perfume, costume, balloon, plume and, I
assume, the groom (the great baboon).

Strewn across the pontoon, flowers in bloom,
cascades a great flume amongst flowering
broom, while guests commune by noon.

By afternoon, we are ready to consume,
by the lagoon, at a table with plenty legroom,
out of nowhere there comes a tune,
and singers begin to croon.

Just as we are given juice of a prune stirred
with a sugar spoon, there is a sudden kaboom.
Soon people swoon in the air of doom.
Surely it's not a typhoon in the midst of June?
How inopportune!

Inside under cover we zoom as black clouds
overhead loom. So dark maroon the moon, one
could presume we were in a tomb, not just a
room in the saloon.

Nothing to Hide

Can't sit still, must do something.
For anyone I'd do everything.
Hate when I can't do anything
Therefore I'm on a hiding to nothing.

To the music I'm dancing
To the beat I'm prancing
To lyrics I'm trying but I can't sing
I'm on a hiding to nothing.

Betraying, staying, decaying, swaying
Whichever Words you are saying
Whatever grand plan you are promising
You're on a hiding to nothing.

Smoking, joking, choking, poking.
Jumping, dunking, honking, thumping.
However you are time wasting.
You're on a hiding to nothing.

Whether revoking or provoking
Whether you're into bling or swing
No matter
You're on a hiding to nothing.

Churn churn churn

In our gut, churn, churn, churn
there is always a reason, churn, churn, churn
A moment to grieve, a moment to heave
A moment to cry, a moment to reason why
A moment to breathe, the moment to leave.

In our gut, churn, churn, churn
there is always a reason, churn, churn, churn
Fear of people, fear of evil
Fear of the journey and fear of being gurney
Fear of what will happen, if we slacken.

In our gut, churn, churn, churn
there is always a reason, churn, churn, churn
A moment of hurt, a moment to blurt
A moment of quiet, a moment to try it
A moment of harmony, a moment of agony.

In our gut, churn, churn, churn
there is always a reason, churn, churn, churn
A lack of strength, clothes the wrong length
A lack of wealth, a dive in your health
Any small noise, interrupts our poise.

In our gut, churn, churn, churn
there is always a reason, churn, churn, churn
Low will power, low self esteem
Low chances of us to follow our dream.
Kept in the dark until we're reached by a light
beam.

In our gut, churn, churn, churn
there is always a reason, churn, churn, churn
Anything can affect us, nothing you can suss
Sometimes we don't want to discuss
Just smile gently and say you believe in us.

Sink or swim

When it's sink or swim time.
When it's time to put the pedal to the meddle.
At the stage of do or die.
You can't predict how you'll cope. Oh no.

It's all I can muster
Always in a fluster
Lost sheen and lacking lustre
Full of bluff and bluster
I'm steadily keeping myself afloat.

When it's sink or swim time.
When it's time to put the pedal to the meddle.
At the stage of do or die.
You can't predict how you'll cope. Oh no.

A message to nobody and everybody
Normal or oddy, neat or shoddy
Never abuse your body
For you only live once, and there's no
replacement to zip into.

When it's sink or swim time.
When it's time to put the pedal to the meddle.
At the stage of do or die.
You can't predict how you'll cope. Oh no.

Challenges come in different shapes and sizes
Different tasks and teases.
Some simple, some impossible
When the body and mind are in pieces.
Strength is how you function throughout.

When it's sink or swim time.
When it's time to put the pedal to the meddle.
At the stage of do or die.
You can't predict how you'll cope. Oh no.

Enough

Sometimes we have enough
Of trying to be tough
When life gets rough
People are gruff
Not understanding your rebuff
Not respecting your stuff
Flattening your fluff
Or seeing through your bluff

A web woven with deception and lies
Spun delicately but well spread to catch flies.
Not my decision, my hands are tied.
Silence broken as I sighed
Limits reached and exceeded, I pleaded
enough.

Enough, enough. I've had enough.
Of trying to be tough
When life gets rough

Happy face is a permanent mask.
Sallow hidden under make-up application.
Nothing can hide the pain in your eyes

The gateway to your soul, they tell no lies.
Limits exceeded, I pleaded enough

Sometimes we have enough
Of trying to be tough
When life gets rough
People are gruff
Not understanding your rebuff
Not respecting your stuff
Flattening your fluff
Or seeing through your bluff

Negative thinking feeds anxious thoughts
Dark depressive words take over
Gaining momentum a few become lots
Whether you are drunk or sober
Limits exceeded, I plead enough!

Chatter

Chatter around us can be either mundane
Or mind numbingly insane
Too loud or so quiet you have to strain.

You do solemnly promise
Never to be dishonest
I promise, honest.

Freedom for a day, so what do you do -
Shop for Balducci and Gucci
Or Dance the hoochie coochie?

Your Daddy is so fabby
His snazzy outfit is very jazzy
As well as the Abbey tabby, who is rather
crabby and flabby.

Sign here, just a squiggle
I'm very good at playing the fiddle
I can't dance, but I can twiddle and jiggle

Chatter around us can be either mundane
Or mind numbingly insane
Too loud or so quiet you have to strain.

Nobody Told Me

Words of wisdom are quiet confessions.
Nobody taught me these life lessons
So I'm going to tell you in this session.
Everyone will learn something here, no matter
their profession.

Nobody told me you should choose carefully
who you trust.
That nobody is perfect, yet we spend our lives
seeking perfection.
That every relationship is a compromise.
Nobody told me as we grow up, our parents
are growing old.

Nobody told me before you are old and wise,
you are young and stupid.
That respect lasts longer than attention.
That nowhere worth going has a shortcut.
Nobody told me the greatest failure of all is not
trying.

Nobody told me you can be comfortable or
courageous - not both.
That what worries you masters you.
That hope anchors the soul.
Nobody told me it's best to count your rainbows
not your thunderstorms.

Nobody told me that impossible is not a fact,
it's an opinion.
Nobody told me our stories are made up of our
struggles.
Nobody told me that the best things happen
unexpectedly.
And definitely, absolutely, nobody told me
everything happens for a reason.

Dance the Flamingo Fandango

Play piano
Pluck a banjo
Sing soprano
Dance the Flamingo Fandango

Everyone can feel the music
You'd tap your feet if you loosened up
The rhythm flows through you
As you're lost in the beat : yep.

Precision and elegance.
Movements of calm grace
The Flamingo Fandango can be slow or fast
Take it at your own pace.

Since I was small
Part of the school choir
I had dreamt of letting loose
Proper equipment and correct attire.

I'm tone deaf
And that ain't ideal.
Nonetheless, I'm determined
The music I'll make is real.
Dance the Flamingo Fandango!

They Said

They said I wouldn't be a success
They said you'll never make it
They said you can try but you'll fail
They speak bullshit.

It's your life
You are your only limit
Decide what your focus is
And go for it, as the law permits.

They said I wouldn't be a success
They said you'll never make it
They said you can try but you'll fail
They speak bullshit.

I've done things in life
I never thought I would
I have a variety of achievements
Most of which, I thought I never could.

They said I wouldn't be a success
They said you'll never make it
They said you can try but you'll fail
They speak bullshit.

You have only one life so live it.
You may only get one chance so grab it.
And never look back with regret
Don't live a life of what if it...

They said I wouldn't be a success
They said you'll never make it
They said you can try but you'll fail
They speak bullshit.

Dreams and Screams

Dreams and screams in my head
Mixing reality with the unreal
Fears and doubts only spread
Don't make of your only chance a meal.

We can beat this
We just need to focus instead
Cut out distractions
Blinkering our vision ahead

Imagination great for creativity
But hard to hold onto a conversation thread
Switch your attention to the now
Try to understand what is left unsaid.

Tasks you've procrastinated over
Those hundreds of messages unread
Leave your head muzzy as if you aren't sober
Fill you with leadened dread.

Dreams and screams in my head
Mixing reality with the unreal.
Sap your strength, but plough on with the
theme
Even if it's only in your head, follow your
dream.

Flustered Mastered

When flustered, I tell myself my courage
should be mustered.
Displeasure upon my face will be plastered.
A poker face I have not mastered.
Under my breath I mutter you bastard.

Colouring the ominous harassed pink
What's wrong - what do you think?!
Take your time, there's no rush
That lie only heightens my blush.

When flustered, I tell myself my courage
should be mustered.
Displeasure upon my face will be plastered.
A poker face I have not mastered.
Under my breath I mutter you bastard.

Negativity cannot be allowed to rule
Or people will continue to play the fool.
Why is positivity so hard to conjure?
At times it's needed for sure.

When flustered, I tell myself my courage
should be mustered.

Unique

You are unique
As is everyone else, no except...
Compliments and critique
We find equally difficult to accept

The attraction of a gadget
For most is like a magnet.
At any budget something for you to fidget
With your only one typing digit.

You are unique
As is everyone else
Compliments and critique
We find equally difficult to accept

Everyone has at least one passion,
Mine include Radleys and jewellery
But unique pieces, nothing in fashion
Boutiques to me are just tomfoolery.

Remember! You are unique
As is everyone else
Compliments and critique
We find equally difficult to accept

What Happened

What happened?
I was approaching my peak
Life was ripe like ready to eat fruit
There was no warning, not even a squeak.

Future plans of mine
Relegated to imaginative flashbacks
What happened to me, and why, and how
No longer able to have life lived to the max.

What happened to time being a healer?
Well, some things won't ever heal.
It's a cruel lesson I've had to learn.
What happened to that footnote?

What happened to my energy; my strength?
Send a postcard to the usual address
If anyone can tell me?
Or if you want to have a guess.

What happened to my brain?
Five seconds ago, what was I doing?
Everything has to be questioned now.
It's driving me insane!

What happened to the belief
Specialists had the knowledge to 'fix' you
Exercises strengthened and improved you
What happens when your belief is shattered?

What happened when you knew
It was too splintered to glue?
What happened when you knew
The truth was biting down hard? And forever?

Failure and Trying

Failure and trying, yes, they go together well.
It can't be a failure if you really were trying.
Trying and failing is better than doing nothing.
Don't sit back and say it, you'll be caught lying.
The only person you're failing is yourself.

A sunk in the middle cake isn't perfect
But it's still edible, it's not really a failure.
An album that doesn't sell out first day
But it's still popular, it's not really a failure.
It can't be a failure if you were really trying.

People rate failure in many a different way
Like work that gets recognition but doesn't pay
Or a perfect manicure that chips after one day
It can't be a failure if you were really trying.

Laughing at your own jokes isn't a failure.
Coming in last at your sport isn't failure.
Missing a personal deadline isn't failure.
Family vehicle not a sports car isn't failure.
A few treats into your diet isn't failure.
It can't be a failure if you were really trying.

Rules

Everyone knows we have rules for a reason.
Safety, sanity, sensibility and stability.
Rule breakers receive a wrist slap or hang for
treason.
Practicality and equality, rules are for us all.
Rules are applicable for every season.

Don't complain. We need the rules.
In work and in schools.
Otherwise we'd be taken for fools.
On the roads in cars, not wagons and mules.
Everyone knows no arguing with the rules.

But... The Devil in each of us whispers,
There's no harm bending them a bit
Cats determine their paths by their whiskers
Surely we too could squeeze a little more?
Rules keep things fair and stop the bickerers.

Loopholes and twisting of rules
To suit you and the occasion
Isn't ever advisable
Despite your powers of persuasion

Okay

I'm okay
As in, okay in the circumstances
Okay for the time being

Okay until something else happens
Okay until the medication wears off
Okay until the darkness surrounds me.

Okay as long as you're not leaving me alone.
Okay as long as there's someone to talk to.
Okay as long as I can be strong.

Okay because of what I have to endure next
Okay because it's all necessary
Okay because there is no choice.

I'm not okay when I think too much.
I'm not okay when pain overtakes my thinking.
I'm not okay when I can barely lift my head
from the pillow.

I'm not okay when pushed beyond my
boundaries.
I'm not okay when you interfere in what's not
your business.

I'm not okay when you tell me I'm overreacting
and pretending.
I'm not okay in the small hours of the longest
nights
I'm not okay in the darkest hours of the longest
days
I'm not okay, not really, but nobody wants to
hear it - so, I'm okay.

Powers of flowers

Roadside summer poppies, and
daffodils blowing gently in the breeze
Lily pollen poison and Venus fly traps
Such extremes in the Powers of flowers.

Herbalists and homeopaths rely upon
The Powers of flowers
A bouquet can bring cheer or despair,
depending on your allergies.

Such powers stretch to weeds
Which are flowers where you don't want them
Flourishing in the tiniest crack of paving
We can learn lots from the powers of flowers!

Thousands of varieties shedding
Thousands of seeds spreading
Daily, weekly, monthly
Bringing surprises when they take root, such
are the Powers of flowers.

The sight of the bright ones
Can lift the darkest of moods.
Even the evergreen
Bring something, such are the Powers of
flowers.

The Black Dog

The black dog is a description of depression.
Like an overexcited puppy, it's hard to push
away for long.
The black dog seems to be a constant in our
shadow.
Perhaps he's black, so not everyone sees him.
He'll blend in for a while, but nose you
Every so often as a reminder he's there.

We may not subconsciously attract him.
We may not subconsciously know how to rid
ourselves of him.
We must make peace with the black dog in our
shadow.

But don't encourage him, he's too boisterous,
he needs to learn to be calm and quiet.
The black dog visits us all.
There's no black magic involved.
He chooses how long he stays.

Blushing and Cussing

Blushing and cussing all the time
One or the other describes me most days.
When things aren't going fine.
There are other ways, I know.

When your free kick hits the wall
At the car park, you are only pence short
When your favourite sandwich sells out
Now you're also blushing and cussing!

Watching your P's and Q's at a gallery
Diet regimes have you counting every calorie
Forced to party when you'd be in the scullery
No wonder you're blushing and cussing.

Blushing and cussing all the time
One or the other describes you most days.
When things aren't going fine.
There are other ways.

Demonics have fun and frolics,
But bollocks, they also make fuck ups.
Compassion in dollops, geed up by wallops.
See? We're all blushing and cussing.

The Edge

You see the edge
I've just teetered over it
Can you see that?
In my face, in my eyes.

On the edge, we seesaw
Maybe for minutes, or hours, or days or longer
Walking the edge is like a tightrope walk.
Shaky and dangerous and ready to tumble at
any moment.

Teetering over the edge
Hanging in midair
Frightened and fearful
Living in despair

Life is not just black and white
Nothing is so clear cut
Amongst the shadows, the light stalks
Throwing out tones of grey darkness and
lightness together

Nothing is easy to come by.
Nothing easy is worth the journey,
Or so they say.
But why is everything so bloody hard?!

Hurt and Hate

Hurt and hate are hand in hand
Why do you hurt the ones who love you?
What makes you drive them away?
Why can't you accept their support?
Depression brain deals only in hurt and hate.

Hurt and hate are hand in hand.
We hurt our loved ones and then hate
ourselves for it.
They hate us for it.
But it's not really us speaking.
Depression brain strikes once more.

Hand in hand, go hurt and hate.
We can't process emotion anymore.
We don't see that end of tunnel light
We see only the darkness of hate
Feel only the pain of hurt, thanks to our
depression brain.

Hurt is so very hard to shake.
Forgive and forget is too.

I'm not sure I can do either of these things.
Positives slip away while negatives grab the
spotlight.
Depression brain only deals in hurt and hate.

Hate this, hate everything
Hate the situation, hate the facts
Hate myself, hate yourself
Hate the pain and the hurt caused.
Hurt and hate kick into high gear.

We must beat the bad thoughts
Battle the blues
Move on from hate
Heal from the hurt
And banish the hate and hurt.

It's too easy to let yourself hurt
It's too easy to let yourself hate
To reprogramme depression brain takes time
But don't stop pushing through.
We can beat hate and hurt.

Words are Weapons

You can easily wound someone with words
Words of cruelty, of mocking, of jest.
Words, once released, cannot be taken back.
Words are weapons.

A nasty word can deliberately upset.
A handful of words of praise raise us up.
Barbed words are a real danger.
Snide remarks behind our backs are as bad.
Words are weapons.

Words without tone are hard to distinguish.
Are they for real or is it used in sarcasm?
Did we understand what the words convey?
Or did we pretend before we knew for sure?
Words are weapons.

Piercing like a sword.
Released as rapid as a shot.
Echo like the death knell on and on in our ears.
The easiest way to hurt someone is to speak.
Words are weapons.

I Do Not Understand

I do not understand
What happened to the woman I knew?
The one who knew me; who understood
And in return I understood her.
I do not understand.

One minute life is a party, everyone is happy.
Then everything changes in a second.
Unhappy and alone - the party carries on
without you.
I do not understand.

You cared about me yesterday.
My words had some worth.
My ideas had weight.
But not anymore - I do not understand.

An illness that cannot be cured.
When everything else has a remedy?
Why can I never catch a break?

Why is it always me? I do not understand.

Turned Tail

You turned tail and ran away,
When you knew it was no good
When you knew it would make no difference
When you knew it'd do more harm than good
Why did you turn tail?

Turned Tail and ran away
From your fears, your pain, your problems
You do know, don't you, that they won't
disappear just because you did.
Why did you turn tail?

I thought you were my soulmate
I thought you were my emergency 2am call
I thought you were my anchor
Why did you let me loose and turn tail?

Why agree when you don't?
Why say things you don't mean?
Why deny yourself, and me, of a simple
pleasure?
Why make it all so much worse for us both?
Why did you turn tail?

Hard Slog

You ask about my day
And I deflect the question
Most of my days are a hard slog
An uphill battle with the ordinary and mundane.
Forgive me of the deflection.
I don't wish to dwell in that world.
Prefer to move on instead.

Nothing is easy anymore.
Nothing isn't complicated anymore.
I use the word plod as it's so apt.
Patience, planning and pacing are vital parts
Of aiding my daily journey of hard slog.

I look jealously at those living a normal life
Enjoying simple things, at times that suits them
Until they discover the hard slog
- but they can step off when they've had
enough. Lucky buggers!

Small things, once complete, are victories.
My battles are never ending,
Thus I avoid what I know I cannot cope with.
Is it self preservation or delaying the inevitable
I'm only trying to ease life's hard slog.

Meeting You

Arranging a meeting with you
I thought it would never come true
It's funny to think as I look across the table
We've known each other so long online
Now, sitting here with me, you are real.

Your genuine smile when we locked eyes
Your welcoming hug, the warmth of your touch
Your smart attire, your practical style
All what I expected and more.

Nothing awkward between us
After all, we are not strangers.
And as I watched you walk away, I knew
We'd arrange another meeting soon.

Sometimes you just click with another person
But at times, no spark is borne.
Sometimes you want it so much you are
blinded by the truth of incompatibility.
And sometimes, it's Fate.

Socially Inept

I'm socially Inept.
A disgrace to society.
Letdown to humankind.
However you say it
The words used do not matter
For they tell the same tale.

I'm socially inept, I know it.
In public, I can't help but show it.
All alone, even in a crowd
Keeping quiet even when the music is loud.
In the dark corner, you'd find me.

Not that I lack intelligence
Not that I lack interest
Not that I radiate hatred
Nor do I pay enough attention
Cos I'm socially inept.

I'm far more interested in you than me
More happy talking to one person than three
I'll answer your questions if I believe you care.
But that I find is rare
Because I'm socially inept.

Weird and Wonderful

Sad that the unusual of us
Are classed as weird and wonderful
With a knowing look, or giggle afterwards.
Don't take any notice of me.
Talk over me like I'm invisible.

You'll learn. You'll see. You'll realise one day.
The world needs us all - Yes, all
Including the weird and wonderful.

We don't have enough time
To learn all of life's lessons
We don't have enough strength
To shoulder the world's problems
Unless we work together
You, him, her, and even me
Although, I am, weird and wonderful.

Nobody Does

I don't like to make a fuss

I don't like to put people out.

But I don't know what to do anymore.

And it seems nobody else does either.

Dying is the only thing we have in common

At the end of our days

Look upon it as a new chapter

A new challenge, a step up.

You'll be flying - no pain or suffering holding you back

Go. Let go. Go now.

The next phase is here.

Take it. Cherish it. Live it. Embrace it.

Don't fear it. Don't worry over it. Take it. It's yours.

Gone

When I'm gone, you'll still be here.
Same things every year.
I hope you are appreciated.
And behind your back you are not slated.

I find it sad.
You're treated so bad
When you deserve so much more.
Never knew you ever swore.

Nobody will remember me
But I shall remember you, to a "T"
Some bastards have no morals.
Sitting resting on their laurels.

You're running the show. The stage is yours.
Without you, we have no spotlight on set.
Cast adrift, onboard a dinghy without oars.

We need you to keep us on course.
You're our power - the only source.
You make it right, you make it fair.
You try, you do, you care.

When Did We Lose Our Sight

When did we lose our sight?
We stopped seeing what was around us, and
only saw ourselves.
We're too wrapped up in our own world to even
look up!
How can we turn our backs on other's blight?

How did we let this happen?
Look for the answer, no matter the question.
We don't know that we aren't always right.
We ignore every other suggestion.
When did we lose our sight?

Did you notice my achievement,
maybe to you it was only slight
Were you there when the time came,
when it was right.
Did you see me smile instead of fight?
    No.
You were lost, in your thoughts, in your mind.
Life, family, work - it's all such a bind.
Even a nod or a smile would have been kind.
When did we lose our sight?

Changes

My handwriting has changed to a scrawl.
Uncomfortable in bed, even curled in a ball.
Daily tasks take so much longer to haul.
My life is not my own, not at all.

From a young age, I had the mentality
To do what I wanted to, when it was a
practicality.
Looking back now, I wonder if actually
I knew then, but just not factually.

I'm having a tough time here
Can anyone spare me a cheer
Instead of the usual down nose sneer?
Or, worse, a disgusted leer?

If you don't know what to say
That's okay.
You can do it your way.
You're not forced to stay.

Try to make me see sense
Give me your two pence (worth)
Your brilliant breakthrough cure
I've heard many times for sure.

Swansong

When I needed help, I didn't ask.
It's not that none of them weren't up to task
Such a vulnerable plea breaks my mask
Further alienating me, as if I'm in a cask.

Frightened more of causing a fuss
Calling myself such a wuss.
Able to fight on was such a plus.
Though, I only relaxed when I sat on the bus.

Two days of resting in bed
And taking the meds like they said
It can't be that bad, as I ain't dead
If Mr Death was near, he soon fled.

When it happens again, things might go wrong.
I might have waited for help too long.
My weak body is still headstrong
This will be my Swansong.

Stride

Take it in your stride.
Your strong shoulders a mile wide
Nobody would dare chide
For you are on everyone's side.

Light Work

Many hands make light work
I ain't heavy
I'm a burden too much
On shoulders already loaded
Thanks to the few
Who pick me up, cheer me up, chivy me.
You know who you are - whether you have
chosen either option.

Carrying

Carrying on, plodding along
Stopping now, at a standstill.
Carrying on is too much now, you see
Holding my own against the tide.
Holding on until strength becomes weakness.

Carrying on holding on, but only just.
I've hit the level of my tolerance.
Even tiniest things are too much.
Heartbroken by the realisation I need carrying
Anyone out there to aid my journey further?
Help me progress until I'm able to resume

Carrying on, plodding along.

Forgive Me

I did my best, I dug in, I knuckled down
But it's never enough - my body let me down
I'm a burden, a disappointment to society
Can't promise anything, can't plan in advance
Washes over me, flicking my off switch
As if my life's achievements do not exist.
Life is a constant battle, pain is my shadow.

Forgive me for not taking it well,
As I reverse into my shell
I sought answers to bring back my life.
Never did I suspect the answer would be
the end of what I enjoyed, what I planned.

It's hard to conceive
The life I put on pause cannot be retrieved.
And as I find techniques and replacements
That safety mat is tugged from me once more.
Proof that no matter what I do I cannot win.

Forgive me for not taking it well,
As I reverse into my shell
I sought answers to bring back my life.
Never did I suspect the answer would be
the end of what I enjoyed, what I planned.

Crud

My name is mud
My body is a dud
Call me a fud
A no good spud
I'm full of crud
Nobody asks for me, I have no bud
There's nothing to see, no blood
Just an internal flood

Treat Me Right

They wouldn't act like this if it was cancer
Instead I'm ridiculed and called a chancer
No specialist can give me an answer
Before I certainly was no dancer
Now I'm a plodder, no longer a prancer.

Keep On

What to do
I don't know anymore
What to say
I don't know anymore
I wish I knew
How the hell to get through
Those who understand are few
We need to stick together like glue

What to do
In order to keep on doing
What to say
In order to keep on going
What to believe
In order to keep on hoping
What to expect
In order to keep on living

How to slow down
When you have only one super speed
How to pace yourself
And recognise its what you need

How to cope
In order to learn to carry on
I wish they wrote a book
So I could always look it up

What to do
In order to keep on doing
What to say
In order to keep on going
What to believe
In order to keep on hoping
What to expect
In order to keep on living

Where's the instructions?
Isn't there a blueprint?
There's a plan to follow right?
Oh. Zilch. Zip. Zero.

What to do
I don't know anymore
What to say
I don't know anymore
I wish I knew

How the hell to get through
Those who understand are few
We need to stick together like glue

Achievement

All achievements are successes.
Achievement meets a goal, hits a target, yes.
These we share because we are blessed.

Achievements can be tiny or tremendous.
Silly or stupendous.
But as long as you achieve something, it's time
well spent.

An achievement in life is a marker
Achievements measure progress
All our achievements we should acknowledge.

Life and love, chance and hope, awards and
achievements,
Each experience teaches us how to cope
With life's joys and bereavements.

Feeling a sense of achievement
Heightens your feeling of being alive
You have made a difference
Now watch it thrive.
When you look back at what you've done
Through life's severity and fun
Will you stop and stay, or keep up the run
Lack of achievement makes you undone

Books by Yvonne Marrs

<u>Introduction to the Fictional Work of Yvonne Marrs</u>

<u>When The Sax Man Plays Part 1 - Making It</u>
<u>When The Sax Man Plays Part 2 - Proving It</u>
<u>When The Sax Man Plays Part 3 - Managing It</u>
<u>When The Sax Man Plays Part 4 - His Return</u>
<u>When The Sax Man Plays Part 5 - The Prequel</u>
<u>When The Sax Man Plays ...and All That Jazz</u>
<u>The 'When The Sax Man Plays' Series</u>

<u>Football Crazy 1: A World Cup Adventure</u>
<u>Football Crazy 2: On The Edge of Glory</u>
<u>Football Crazy 3: The Hat-trick</u>
<u>Football Crazy 4: A Point to Prove</u>
<u>Football Crazy 5: The Master of Managerial Psychology</u>
<u>The 'Football Crazy' Series</u>

<u>Aiden Lewis Octet Book 1 - Memoirs</u>
<u>Aiden Lewis Octet Book 2 - Reminiscence</u>
<u>Aiden Lewis Octet Book 3 - Touring</u>
<u>Aiden Lewis Octet Book 4 - Bravado</u>
<u>Aiden Lewis Octet Book 5 - Partnership</u>
<u>Aiden Lewis Octet Book 6 - Vulnerable</u>
<u>Aiden Lewis Octet Book 7 - Struggles</u>
<u>Aiden Lewis Octet Book 8 - Denouement</u>
<u>The 'Aiden Lewis Octet' Omnibus</u>

<u>Undeserved 1</u>
<u>Undeserved 2</u>
<u>Undeserved 3</u>

We hope you have enjoyed this book, please leave a review for Yvonne.

9 798215 359952